Sophia's Medicine

Weaving Bridges In Divided Times

By

Dr Elizabeth Undine

ISBN (paperback colour): 978-1-9161547-0-4

ISBN (paperback black&white): 978-1-9161547-2-8

ISBN (epub): 978-1-9161547-1-1

For My Son.
Forgive my clichés, but please do remember
to try to *remember*
and in the meantime
try not to forget
no clouds… no rain… no flowers…
Love always.
Mom, Mum, Mam.

Chapters

Introduction

IN TIMES GONE by, human beings lived, loved and lost in two interconnected worlds; the physical world *and* the imaginal world. We were cave dwellers and cloud dancers. Our minds, bodies, spirits and souls harmoniously flowed in a balanced state of communion; both with ourselves, and with all others.

Now, in this era of technological wizardry, in this exalted period of intellectualism, we are 'educated' to recognise the physical world—the material world—as the only 'real' world. Mind and reason are idolised, as are the *youthful* appearances of our flesh and blood physical bodies. We still tend to bestow spirit a piecemeal recognition (albeit grudgingly), but soul has been scathingly rejected by the vocal majority. The very existence of soul has been contemptuously ridiculed and our soul connections, ruthlessly severed. We are unbalanced, unhinged and soul separated—dangerously so. We need to evolve, again. We can't go back; we can only go forwards. But in order to do that, first we must remember, then we must reclaim—and for that, we shall return to the Beginning…

1

Once upon a *time* (*exactly* 13.8 billion years ago, or approximately 6 thousand years ago—depending on particular perspectives and *in no way* limited to the preceding two options) there was *the Beginning*. Perhaps, it would be more legitimate to say, it was simply *a* beginning; merely one amongst a seemingly infinite number of parallel first moments, but as this is a story (and a somewhat mercurial story at that), it shall start where it wants: with a bang. A fantastically *Big Bang*; and with *the Word*.

In the Beginning
was the Word
and the Word
was a sound.

In the Beginning
was a sound
and then sound
became wave.

Wave
became form
and then form
became
you.

You
are the wave
and the sound
and the Word.

You
are a drop
in the ocean
of divinity.

One
with the song
dancing into
infinity.

2

BEFORE THE BEGINNING, there existed (or did not exist) only the Unknowable: everything *and* nothing; everywhere *and* nowhere.

In the Beginning, an emanation of the Unknowable inverted *into* Time and Space; and "*Boom!*"—or should we say, "*Bang!*"—the Word was born.

After the Beginning, *in* Time and Space, the Word multiplied. One became Two; Two became Four, and so on and so forth. New words were formed: words like *you*, and words like *me*. Words like good and bad; right and wrong; love and hate.

Words came together in lines. Sentences joined one another and became stories: stories like *this* story; stories like *your* story.

In Time and Space, however, the word became here *and* there. The word became past, present *and* future, and so stories were divided (or in error, believed themselves to *be* so).

Separation led to *fear* and fear caused stories to fold in upon themselves; to contract; to grow skins and to build walls.

The Wall

Who built this wall
between the trees
cleaving
our worlds;
you
or me?

Towering stone
too high to scale.
I know
I tried
and failed.

On the other side
I feel you there
close by
yet
unaware.

So I must go
my mind is made.
Too dark
and cold
in this
cruel
shade.

Or should I stay
just one day more
and try
again
to find
the door?

3

THERE ARE PATHS across the gaps; ways to bridge the separations; doors built into our dividing walls.

But what if finding a door is still not enough?

Clenched fist
keeps on knocking
but the door
remains
closed.
Knuckles
bloody
swollen
body slumps
to the floor.

Sleet
lashes down.
Desolation
takes hold.
No shelter
to be found.
No shelter
from *this* cold.

Surrounding good people
their demands
draining.
Painful
conformity
it's clamour
deafening.

Retreat
to recoup.
Dark night
reveals sight
ablaze
from your window

Closed Door

a burning
bright light!

Beg
to come in.
Bended knees
implore.
Deafness.
Deadbolt.
'Keep Out'
on your door.

4

WHAT CAN A simple story do, when faced with seemingly insurmountable obstacles?

This story grew wings.

P.S. Don't automatically diagnose an underlying Angelic-Identification Disorder. There's more than one winged myth flying around. Just consider Icarus... pretty messy.

Swimming below
I feel you
above
and reach for you.

Flying above
I see you
below
and fall for you.

Why fall at all?

You're lost
in the darkness.
I know the way

and
I love
fish.

Cormorant

Cormorant

5

IN TIME AND Space stories forget *what* they are, *who* they are and *where* they are.

Most stories forget completely.

But some do not.

Rock pool
lies
upon
the shore.
A part
of
the shore?

Before
she was
a part
of
the ocean
now
she is
a-part
from
the ocean.

Did she choose this
this current
stagnant
form?

Who knows?

All *she* knows
is
she's longing
for
a storm.

Rock Pool

All she knows is she's longing for a storm. Did she choose this, this current stagnant form! Who knows. Before she was a part of the oceon, now she is a—part from the oceon. A part of the shore. Rock pool lies upon the shore?

6

SOME STORIES DO succeed in breaking through the veils of forgetting, and in time they find themselves remembering. Remembering sounds like it should feel good, doesn't it?

Trickster medicine
hard to swallow
tastes bitter
vile.
'Do I really have to take this shit?'
Throat spasms
I gag
retch up bile.

You give me another
shards of glass.
'Mirror, mirror
on the wall
who can eat you
best of all.'

I bleed
inside
as slivers
descend.
Cutting.
Slicing.

Senseless destruction
or sly divine genius?

Who knows
the answer
lost
as pain washes over
wave upon wave.

Dying
to know
where

Trickster Medicine

oh where
is my spoon-full
of sugar?

7

If at some point in time a story does remember (at least some of) what has been forgotten, does the pattern of its former twisting story-line now suddenly make sense?

Does this awakened knowledge make *living* its confusing plot any easier?

This madness
is a forest fire
blazing
through my mind.
Consuming all irrelevancies
petty distractions
silly fancies.

I cannot begin to control it
only gaze
in wonder
and awe.
Guess
at the unknown direction
of this unstoppable force
this raging inferno.
Observe
as flames obliterate all
from view;
peak,
then subside.

Leaving stillness
descending peace
amidst
the devastation.
Calm.
Cooling.
Rain.
Falling.

See tender green shoots
reach up
in clearings
where moonlight now

breaks through.
In openings
where before
dense thorny scrub
obscured the fertile soil
from her soft
loving
view.

STORIES ARE NOT finished polished products.

Story-making is an ongoing process, occurring *now* and happening here.

My metal has been tested
found wanting;
weak
malleable
with a promising glimmer
of potential.

Fire rages.
Purify me.
Burn away my sins
victimhood
self-absorption
cowardice.

Now water
unexpected
shockingly cold.
Contrast inverts me
inside out.
Makes up-down
right-wrong.

Perspective flipped
I reel with vertigo.
Strike out at the guiding hand.

Plunged back to the flame
again and again.
Metal strengthens.
Blade sharpens.
Point
found.

Am I ready for battle
or has the hardest battle

already been fought
in preparing
for readiness?

Ego sulks
a petulant bully.
Waits for me to relax my focus.
I *must not*
relax
my focus.

9

SOME CHAPTERS IN a story are undoubtedly more difficult to write (and to read) than others. If a story had a choice would it erase these chapters? Would it rewrite its story, or does a full story—a story with layers, a story with depth—know that these chapters are actually the best ones; that these chapters are the ones that have been essential in (and responsible for) bringing the story to life?

If you'd never
passed through me
would I
have passed through life
as a seasoned traveller
flying everywhere
yet
settling nowhere
and
declaring nothing?

For you
at times
(it felt like)
I gave up
everything.

Yet
from you
I find
I received
it all.

Passing Through

10

25

DOES ANY ONE individual story really matter? Does it matter what a single lone story has to say? Does it matter that some stories remember (aspects of) *where* they came from, *who* they are; and that some do not? Does it matter that some stories strive so hard to dismantle the separating walls, to weave bridges across the illusionary divides, whilst others appear to do only the opposite? Who can say? Can this story say, standing where she stands? Can you say, standing where you stand? Can the children say, the children who can only *try* to stand on this divided, fractured land?

Dead Man Walking

I see a dead man walking.
Dead men
all walking by.
Black orbs for eyes
they look *through* me
and with their smiles
do lie.

I see a woman walking.
Dead women
walking by.
Perfect clothes and painted masks
can't hide
the stains
inside.

I see a dead child walking.
Dead children
walking by.
Too late by far
to say
I'm sorry
or sins
to justify.

The swan
looks on
in horror
at the people
passing
by.
She tells the water
tells the grasses
tells the trees
who tell
the sky.

27

SOMETIMES EVEN A story cannot find the right words to tell her tale.

I'm supposed to be
good with words
(so they say)
yet
here I sit
(again)
unable to speak;
my mouth
a vacant chamber
my lips
a clasping gate.

Within me
fall drops of gentle rain
holding such sweetness
just a few would make the whole desert
bloom.
Each pearl
a melody
a touch
a kiss
a soothing balm for weeping wounds.

If I can't speak
just yet
then you must
come closer.
Come to my quiet shores
and bathe
your tired
aching
feet.
Undress
slip into warm waters
and sink
into the depths
of me.

12

WHAT ARE THE children saying? What are they saying about the distorted stories we strain to shape them into; about the fake plastic covers we wrap around them; about the suffocating bindings we tie them into; and about the callously soiled pages we bequeath as their shameful, dirty inheritance?

Can you *hear* what the children are saying? The children are speaking.

The question is, are *we* listening?

The Pied Piper

About once a month
(more often more)
we admit a child
to my children's ward.
A child who's failed
(thankfully so)
to take their own life
to end
it all.

Foiled leaving attempts
I pray
they'll all know
for if one succeeds
there's no end
to that sorrow.

'Failed child suicide'
has become common
and common
becomes
normal.

'Failed child suicide'
has become
normal
and the horror's
right there!

The *unthinkable*
is now
normal.

The Pied Piper

We're down
a dark mine
and caged songbirds
are falling.

The frog's
in the pan
and the water
is boiling.

The pied piper
is playing
his flute
softly
calling
as he lures
our *own* children
not-so-gently
away.

What music
can *we* play
to convince them
please
stay.

13

THE TIME HAS come for change—deep transformative change, not fake white-washing gimmickry. If not in time for this story, if not in time for you, then at least for the sake of the children and their children…

But whom should a story trust *to say* what needs to be said? Whom should a story trust *to do* what needs to be done? Should a story delegate this responsibility to another—and if she did, whom should it be? Should she choose one from among our current 'chosen few': a corporate crony, a jaded judge, a puppet politician, or a billionaire businessman?

Should she? Would you?

Who will speak for the trees?

Can earth
speak
for the trees;
earth that embraces tree's roots?

Can water
speak
for the trees;
water that suffuses tree's body?

Can air
speak
for the trees;
air that caresses tree's form?

Can light
speak
for the trees;
light that loves and loves and loves each
blessed green leaf?

Would you trust the woodcutter
to speak
for the trees?
The merchant
who measures their worth
in pounds
of flesh?

Would you bring the woodcutter
to the Sacred Grove
and listen

enchanted
as he talks
his talk
and sit
entranced
as he raises
his
axe?

P.S. No INSULT to genuine 'woodcutters' intended! This story has taken no small liberty with metaphors. Please forgive her—for this and for other, perhaps more unwitting, word appropriation crimes, past and future.

14

35

RATHER THAN LOOKING outwards and judging others, should this story instead direct her gaze inwards, and concentrate on editing her own glaring mistakes?

P.S. IT WOULD take a long time indeed; they are legion.

Is your love
like the lighthouse
or
is your love
like the moon?

Round
and round
this question
would go.

Now I know
the *real* question
is;
is my love
like the lighthouse
or
is my love
like the moon?

And why is it
I have to fight
so hard
not to hurt
those I love
so?

15

37

This story sees how she places conditions on other stories.

Unconditional

You
give me
that
then request
of me
this.

I
resist.

I
give you
this
then insist
of you
that.

You
react.

Yet
there you are
breathing.

And
here I am
breathing.

And
here we are
receiving.

16

39

SHE SEES HOW misunderstandings *between* stories so easily occur.

I
say *this*.

You think
I mean
that.

You
say *that*.

I think
you mean
this.

How can you hear
my
this?

How can I hear
your
that?

The Silence
receives
our this
and that.

The Silence
gives back
our this
and that.

Misunderstandings

17

Sometimes, this story feels overwhelmed by the task she is attempting: to form a bridge, a bridge between divided worlds; fractured worlds of different words; words like science and words like soul; words like knowledge and words like knowing. Such apparently irreconcilable worlds, of separate divided words. How can she possibly succeed in this seemingly impossible mission, when she sometimes finds she can't even piece together another simple sentence?

Running On Empty

I'm running on empty
my tank is so dry
so painfully depleted
display dials lie.

I'm driving on fumes
I'm freewheeling downhill
can't slow this momentum
could easily kill.

Brakes worn away
disc pads squealing
handbrake slipping
paint sadly peeling.

Design outdated
light bulbs blown
seats badly stained
dents disowned.

Gearbox snagging
clutchwire snapped
electrics malfunctioning
suspension collapsed.

Battery drained dead
windows cracked-broken
steering wheel twisted
doors won't open.

I'd drown out the evidence
with old '80's hits
but speakers are smashed

and stereo's been nicked.

I detest this mess
rusted wreck I've become
scrapheap's blessing
what more can be done?

A mechanic won't do
it's too late for that
but Sophia's elixir?
Well perhaps, just perhaps.

18

44

THIS STORY DOES admit that at times, she has really wanted to bring her tale to a premature last full-stop.

No more words
no more poems
to feed these tears
that keep on flowing.

I'm torn in two
I'm torn apart
I cannot mend
this fractured heart.

I want to stop
I want to bend
the hands of time
into the end.

The circle's woven
the circle's spun
I've played my part…
let me come home.

19

SHE DOES NOT know how her tale can be heard in time, or how she can discuss with compassion the insidious disease that wants to stay hidden, but what needs to be seen if we wish to survive, never-mind, eventually thrive.

Are we
(in part at least)
the cancer
we so lament
afflicting us?

Lung metastasis.
Stealer of breath.

Are we the bony-pain
gnawing through
broken
sleepless
nights?

Pathological fracture.
Support structure collapsed.

Are we the toxins
poured into
life-giving waterways?

Artery polluting.
Blood poisoning.

Sapper of energy. Invader of sacred
spaces. Slayer of innocence. Callous
indifference. Unstoppable flow. Growth
that knows no bounds. Lump, limp, itch,
discharge, blindness, paralysis.

Are we the flaw, weakness, fault line
and will we
inevitably crack
but in our breaking

may be given a choice—
surrender
to the truth
and bear
our own witnessing;
or
hold fast
to the lie
and share
in our extinguishing?

20

49

Why do we often wait, until it's simply too late?

Blackbird

Why is it
we seem to
need to
lose our hearts
be torn apart
before seeing
the gifts
we've been given?

Every night
blackbird sleeps
his head
tucked under
wing.

And every dawn
he wakes anew
and sings
and sings
and sings.

21

51

Sometimes, even a story needs to lose herself, before she can find herself again.

Air rushes
I am lost in her breath.

Fire rages
I am consumed in her flames.

Water floods
I am drowned in her depths.

Earth enfolds
I am enveloped in her darkness.

Light caresses
I am revealed as without substance
formless
emptiness
and there
I find myself
as you.

Losing Myself

22

53

This story wasn't sure whether to include this next chapter, but Little One asked to be heard; asked for this part of her too-brief, cut-short story to be told. How could this story possibly refuse her?

The "Drop-Kick" (1)

Vibrating air particles
pause
become still
listen
observe the pivotal moment
as time slows
and the unseen referee
prepares to blow
the final
whistle.

Your muscles were no doubt
tense
with anticipation.
Whole body
poised
for the decisive shot.
Hands
clenching the weight
firmly.
Did they shake
as you tipped over?
Blood racing
heart pounding
ears ringing.
Surrounding sound drowned
by the roaring of an absent
cheering
crowd.

One final bounce
last ounce of pressure on your bent sole
then you release
and drop
the six-kilogram-weight

and kick
making brief
though binding contact
with the dorsum
of your off-side
foul-committing foot.

What were you wearing?
I wonder.
Nothing? Did it hurt?
Slippers? Probably not.
Boots? Possibly
though not a rugby field
nor a football field
underfoot
for this conclusive
match
point.

Did you forget?
Did you simply forget
where
you were
who
not 'what'
who...
who you were holding?
Had she already flown when you
"drop-kicked" her
into
the living room wall
and watched her
slip silent
crumpled rag doll
to the floor?

It's the "drop-kick" bit
that somehow sticks.
Your words
lead slivers
buried deep
inside my mind.
And I can't extract them
if I can't see them
and I can't see them
if I can't believe them.

I met you a week before.
Do you remember?
I remember.
I remember her breathing
her perfect heart
beating.
I remember my hand on her chest
her four-month-old chest
and the look in her eyes as she looked into mine.

Have you ever seen
an angel?
I have.
And yes
you have too.
Only
I've never
killed
an angel.
How about you?

The "Drop-Thick" (2)

I've been trying
(or trying not)
to write
(or not write)
about what you said
("drop-kicked")
about what you did
(murder)
to her.

Every word
I write
about that night
comes out wrong.

But how could
any word
I write
about *that* wrong
turn out right?

The "Drop-Thick" (2)

23

58

THIS STORY WOULD like to believe that 'evil' as an independent autonomous entity does not actually exist—that it is not a 'real thing'. Would that not be better/nicer?

But what if evil *does* exist, and that evil itself would also like us to believe that 'it' does not really exist?

Or have we got it all back to front, or upside down? Is it *our* believing *in* evil that *creates* evil?

Like it or not, we all have shadows, dark sides. This story does not believe that these are evil in-and-of themselves, but could it be that evil *lives and hides* in the *denial* of our own shadows? Does evil thrive in the denial and displacement of *our own* darkness?

The Master of Lies

Is The Bad Man real?
Is he?
Isn't he?

I don't *know* so
but do I
sense so?

I don't see him
but do I
feel him
festering
in the divides?
Sickly smiling
in divisions
between truth
and the lies
we hide
inside?

The Master of Lies

24

THIS STORY ADMITS that she does sometimes sound horrible—even to her own ears. She does not mean to, but she is a full story—a story that has lived and loved and lost—and her wounds are part *of* her story; part of the gifts she has to give.

"Write a poem about love"
(I was told).
About love?
What do I know about love?
About loss
pain
grief
betrayal?
About anger
sadness
darkness
despair?

"Are you bitter?"
(I was asked).
Do I *sound* bitter?!
They put lemons in my water
then I was shaken
(not stirred).
I fizzed with rage!
Now
you come
and pour in your sweetness
and together
we seem to have made
lemonade.

It tastes so good.
I didn't realise
I was so thirsty
yet so longing
to be drunk
to be consumed
to be plunged into
as if my being

were an oasis
in a scorching desert
for a wandering
lost
soul.

Drink me
and I will fill you
and in my giving away
be released
to flow
into
complete
sweet
emptiness.

Come taste our lemonade.

25

63

THIS STORY WISHES to speak kindly, to touch lovingly; but the gentle way, alas, is not always the easy way.

Fairy Walking

I want to walk
as do fairies
make
not a sound
flowery feet
falling
kissing
the ground.

But try
as I might
I am clumsy
unsteady
past wrongs
of forefathers
on shoulders
lie
heavy.

26

If this story cannot tread lightly, perhaps she can reach through.

Reaching Through

I want to reach through
touch you
with delicate words
that whisper
like silk
against your receptive skin.
Cherry blossom
falling
from within.
Instead of a black heavy staff
hammering my point across
this space
between us.

I feel an irresistible urge
to lay
these ephemeral thoughts down
as enticing fine lines.
Circular web
weaving you
into
centre point.

Is it because
I have something
immeasurably important
to say
or
is it because
like the divine beloved
my soul longs for
this moment
of connection
with you?

27

67

IF THIS STORY does fail to find the gentle way, perhaps she can find another way: her own way.

We've lost our way.
Sold
our old ways.
Sought
a new way.
Bought
the wrong way.
Gone astray.

Can we turn this course around
reclaim
our old ways
with
the new ways
walk
our own way
with
your way *in* my way
and
my way *in* your way?

One day
maybe
I pray.

28

69

THIS STORY WANTS to share herself; to be of genuine service. This often feels far easier said than done.

I want to serve
but I don't know how.
I only know
it begins
right now.

I long to serve
but what do I do?
I only know
it begins
with you.

It begins right here
but the way
is unclear.
My path is obscured
blocked
by my fear.

Surrender to fear
step *into*
my pain.
Make space for love
to come round
again.

29

71

Sometimes, a story can misplace her own place *in* the story.

Lost in Time

Sometimes
I find
when I'm asleep
I'm awake.

Sometimes
I find
when I'm awake
I'm asleep.

Some-times
I find
I can't find
Time
I can't find
I
in
Time.

30

PERHAPS THIS STORY sounds familiar? Perhaps she does. Perhaps this story is repeating herself, or retelling a story that sounds just like this story, or repeating the same words, or series of similar words, in an annoying, somewhat irritating, repetitive way? Perhaps she is.

Perhaps
I'm saying
the same thing
over
and over
again.

Perhaps I am.

Perhaps
the same thing
needs
to be said
over
and over
again.

Perhaps it does
or
perhaps not.

Perhaps
I should say it
just once.

What would I say?
Would I say
'Wake up!'?
Would I say
*'You are loved beyond all conceivable
measure'*?

Or
if the tone
is just

so
and
the timing
just
right
does one of those
inevitably
break through
into
the other?

And then
two
may become
one
so that
one
can become
two
ad infinitum.

31

Or is this story simply going around in circles?

Spiral Spell

Each spiral
is a spell.

Woven
with words.

Silent
soul echoes.

Whispering
through worlds.

Spiral Spell

Spiral Spell

32

Does a story change depending on who is reading the story? Do the words reshuffle and rearrange on the page? Do the sentences and paragraphs bend to please and appease? Is it the same story from one reading to another? Does it swap its script when the covers are closed? Censor its content for fear of exposure? Tone down its language in anticipation of ridicule?

A story is surely supposed to stay true to itself. It says what it says. It is what it is. Can you say the same of you? Can this story say the same of herself?

Am I
the same I
for all people?
And by *I*
do I know
what I mean?
You see the measure
of my difference
for different people
is a measure
of my distance
from me.
And as I
am so different
for different people
so do I
lie so far
from
me.

33

Where does a story end and the story-teller begin?

Or is that the wrong question entirely?

Yesterday
I stood upon
the gallery floor
seeing
each painting
observing
each scene.

Or did I?

Looking back
I seem to see
a series
of scenes
of me
standing upon
the gallery floor
being seen
by each
painting
being observed
by each
scene.

The Gallery

The Gallery

Yesterday I stood upon the gallery floor, observing a series of scenes, each painting, each scene seen by each painting. Looking back, I seem to see each painting upon the gallery floor, being observed by each scene. Or did I? — standing upon the gallery floor, being seen by each painting, a series of scenes of me, seeing —

34

Some of the pages of this story were at some point *in* time lost, or hidden, or stolen. They're now being returned; but by who, or by whom, or by what?

Who creates the poems?
Not 'I'.
The poems are all
'just there'
conjuring themselves
briefly
as if out of
thin air.
Waiting patiently
(or not)
to be lured closer
or
luring me
closer
close enough
to reach up
and gently ease down
a word
a phrase
a line
a verse
a poem
a mystery?

They catch me
unawares
when the edges blur
or
when I'm tired
drifting off
to the other place
or
busy rushing
with an endless list of things to do
and I say

Writing Poetry (1)

'not now'
or
'later'
but then thankfully succumb
knowing that
later
the mist
will have vanished
the ghost poem
will be gone
exorcised
by neglect
leaving only
dissolving vaporous trails
and
a vague aching memory
of a song
unsung
of a story
untold.

Between three-twenty-three
and three-twenty-four
the knockers came knocking
upon my side door.
I'd left the door open
I'd failed to take care
and they stole your soft breath
right out of
thin air.

I'd fallen asleep and when stirred had
protested
slipped under the covers
guiltily
rested.
When I'd woken
I'd reached out
felt
only loss.
The presence
of emptiness
your gift
that I'd lost.

Bedroom now empty
but haunted
no doubt.
Ghost poem;
it lingers
words whisper about
'You failed to uphold
a promise
you made
but I love you
I'll love you
'til the end of all days'.

Writing Poetry (2) For the Poem That I Failed

The original is gone
but here lies another
an epitaph
of absence
to its sister
or brother.
Potential unknown
guardian's miscarriage stain
lies enshrined on this page
to 'The Poem'
that I failed.

35

THIS STORY APPRECIATES that her words will be unpalatable (putting it mildly) to many.

Apple
lies
discarded
upon
the ground.

Because
she was judged
not-good
or
because
she was judged
not good—
enough?

Did the fault
lie
in her—
she fell down
not
up?

And did worm
first
appear
before
or
after?

36

91

WORDS ARE CERTAINLY powerful; they can even be magical, but does the *real* power and magic of words only unfold in the reading, and speaking, and listening of words *with* another?

Lying here
the untouched paper
aching
for the pen.
Longing
to be written over
to be pressed down upon
by your silver
fountain
point.
Imprinted
with dark flowing ink
leaving
indelible patterns
forever traced
upon naked
parchment
skin.
Carefully
write yourself
over me.
Tenderly
read yourself
back to me.
Then quickly
burn me!
Let my light escape me.
Let my essence be devoured
by the roaring fire
by the raging flames
by the ravenous void
within her gaping
ecstatic
expanse.

37

93

Has this story been alone on her journey?

In the past she may have believed herself so, but not now. Now, she knows… otherwise.

South asks me to claim her
to own my body for her.

West asks me to feed her
to feel and flood for her.

North asks me to know her
to find me and be for her.

East asks me to trust her
to surrender and flow for her.

And in giving myself to them
I'm really giving myself to me.

For the gift is in the giving
and the receiving is the returning.

The Four Directions

38

95

SOME MIGHT SAY that a good story should have a beginning, a middle and of course, an obvious end. This story might disagree. Not just because she likes to disagree; which of course she does (which self-respecting story likes to be told what to do!), but also because she might have to disagree on the whole 'ending' fixation.

But if you still *really* want one, then here it is:

'And they all lived happily ever after' (or perhaps not).

The River

Surrendering
the River Nile
flows through
the estuary.

As I flow freely
into
you
and you
flow into
me.

Where does the sea
become
the river
the river
become
the sea?

Divided form
unbound
dissolves
as waves
wash over
me.

The River

The River

The River

39

Bon Voyage.

P.S. If you do find yourself in any way confused by *Sophia's Medicine* ("what on Earth was that supposed to be!"), this story does sympathise with you. You *have* been led round in circles, but remember, the author did give her word: this book would contain no peddling of hope-filled empty promises, no pledges of healing, no prescriptions for health, and no yellow-brick-road to wholeness. And consider; if at this particular juncture, you *had* been able to categorise, compartmentalise, rationalise, quantify, describe, explain, or simplify the essence of *Sophia's Medicine*, into an identifiable, objectifiable, recognisable or reproducible form, would that not instead have been the *true* storytelling (or soul) transgression?

And perhaps if this story were to tarry any longer, it might accidentally slip up and trespass into real horror territory: The Land of Unwanted Advice Giving! Arghh! So the following isn't advice (honest), but merely a little optional sideways shimmy: if you do become aware of any particularly strong thoughts, emotions or sensations, surfacing during your reading of *Sophia's Medicine* (especially those of a traditionally labelled 'negative' nature), then why not try pressing an imaginary 'pause' button. Stay with those responses, no matter how uncomfortable. *Sink down into* them and see where they lead. Or instead, try imagining yourself standing in front of a large mirror. Gently hold those responses in your hands. Look deeply into the mirror. Let it reflect back to you. What do you see? Where are you? What exactly *is* it, that is provoking this particular reaction? Something in the story, something in the poems, or something in you?

An empty page holds such potential. The journey's all yours now; it always *was*, always *is* and always *will be*.

Write away my friend, write *a way*.

Author Bio

ELIZABETH UNDINE IS a forty-something year old doctor currently practising paediatric medicine in the UK.

Contact her at:
    @Sophia'sMedicine (Twitter)
    or
    elizabethundine@gmail.com

Art work created using print letter cut-outs, recycled from British Medical Journals. #alchemicalart.

10% of Sophia's Medicine book sale profits will be gifted directly to a conservation or other appropriate reader voted charity. Votes & results published on Twitter.

Cast your vote. Have a say. Play a part.

www.ingramcontent.com/pod-product-compliance
Lightning Source LLC
Chambersburg PA
CBHW050958050726
47592CB00007B/2626